Special Shih Tzus

A COLOURING BOOK FOR ADULTS

MW00958677

Paws for Thought: Vol. 10

Christine Vencato

This book is dedicated to my wonderful family

Illustrations and design © 2017 Christine Vencato

www.arttherapycolouringbook.org

First edition; first printing

All rights reserved. No part of this book may be reproduced or copied except
for your own personal, home use - limited to simple reproduction through
photocopy and scan/print. You may not scan into electronic form for the purpose
of distribution without the express permission from the copyright holder.

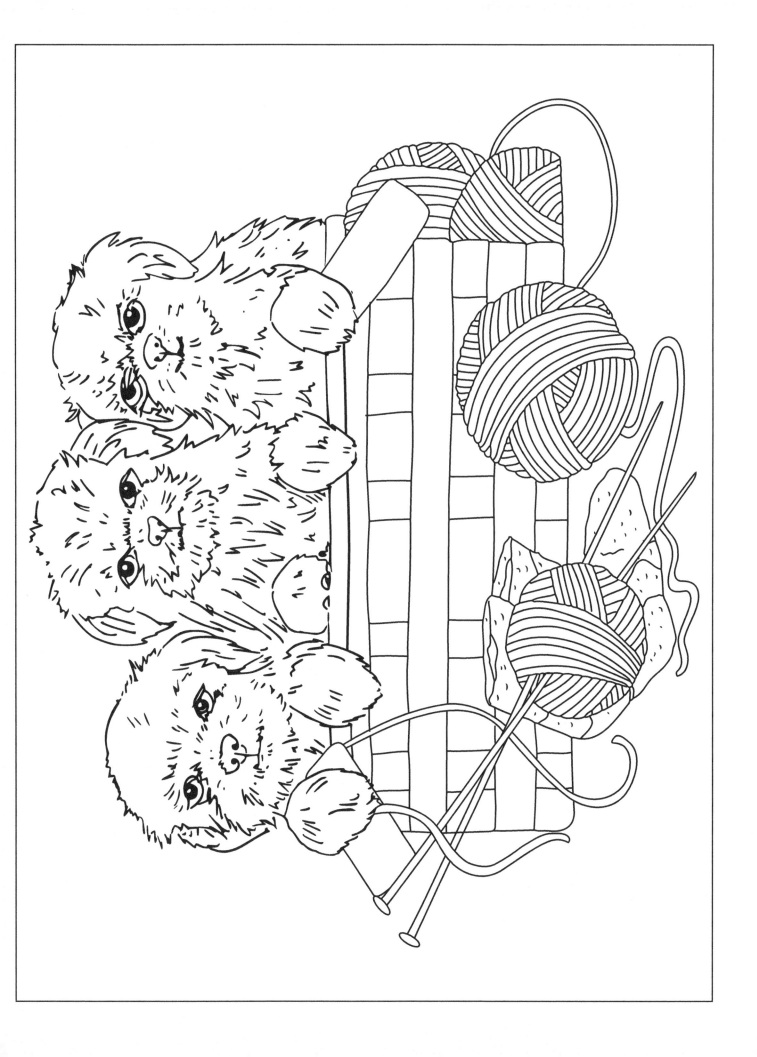

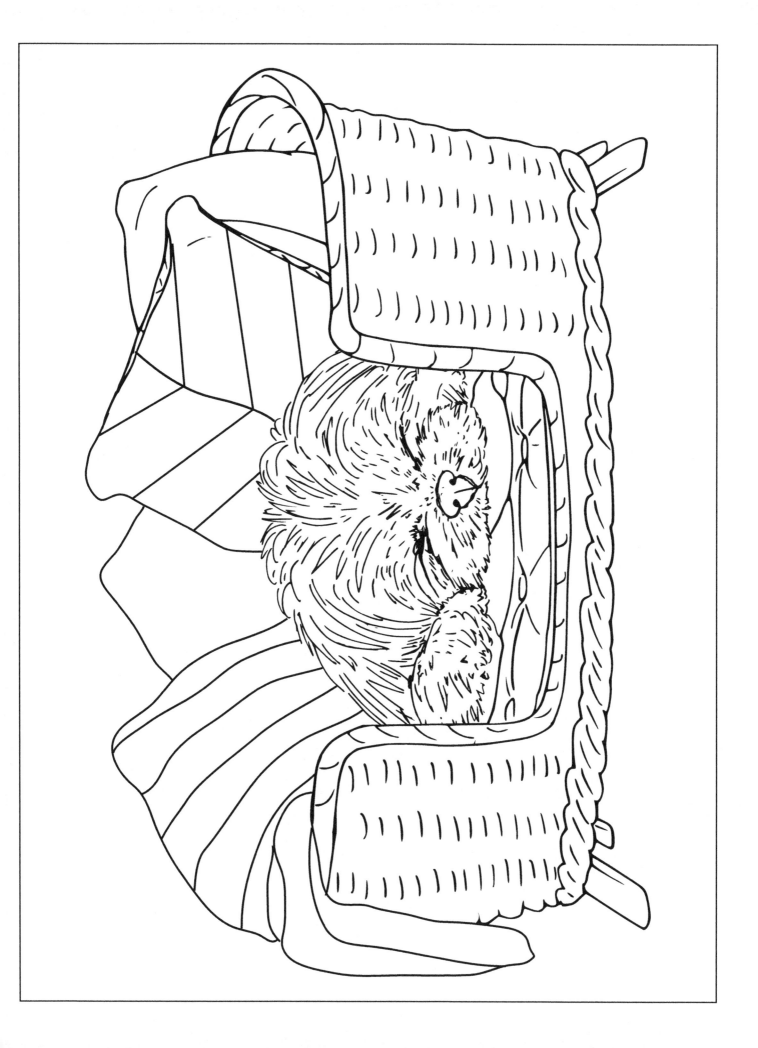

Please visit www.arttherapycolouringbook.org for more information and other titles in the "Paws For Thought" series:

16700753R00044

Made in the USA
Middletown, DE
24 November 2018